MUG RECIPE COOKBOOK

50 SIMPLE AND FLAVORFUL MICROWAVE RECIPES

NAOMI LAWRENCE

COPYRIGHT © [2024] BY [NAOMI LAWRENCE]

All rights reserved. No part of this publication may be reproduced, distributed, or transmitted in any form or by any means, including photocopying, recording, or other electronic or mechanical methods, without the prior written permission of the publisher, except in the case of brief quotations embodied in critical reviews and certain other noncommercial uses permitted by copyright law

TABLE OF CONTENT

TABLE OF CONTENT 3

INTRODUCTION 7

CHAPTER ONE 8

    What are mug recipes? 9

    Tips for Making Nice Mug Meals 10

    Materials Needed To Make Mug Meals 12

CHAPTER TWO: MUG RECIPES 14

    Classic Mug Brownie 15

    Blueberry Muffin in a Mug 16

    Loaded Baked Potato Mug 17

    Spinach and Feta Mug Omelette 18

    Mug Pizza 19

    Chocolate Chip Cookie in a Mug 20

    Mug Banana Bread 21

    Mug Egg Fried Rice 22

    Peanut Butter Mug Cake 23

    Cheesy Broccoli Mug Casserole 24

        Mug Pumpkin Pie 25

- Caprese Mug Scramble 26
- S'mores Mug Cake: 27
- Cinnamon Roll in a Mug 28
- Chicken Alfredo Mug Pasta 29
- Mug Lemon Poppy Seed Muffin 30
- Mac and Cheese in a Mug 31
- Mug Chicken Pot Pie 32
- Raspberry Mug Pancake 33
- Mug Tuna Noodle Casserole 34
- Mug Coffee Cake 35
- Caprese Mug Pasta 36
- Mug Taco Soup 37
- Mug Apple Crisp 38
- Mug Ramen 39
- Mug Quiche Lorraine 40
- Red Velvet Mug Cake 41
- Mug Vegetable Stir-Fry 42
- Mug Cheesecake 43
- Mug Mediterranean Couscous 44
- Mug Key Lime Pie 45

Mug Shrimp Scampi 46

Mug French Toast 47

Mug Chicken Enchilada 48

Mug Pesto Pasta 49

Mug Chocolate Pudding 50

Mug Margherita Pizza 51

Mug Sweet and Sour Chicken 52

Mug Blueberry Cobbler 53

Mug Chicken and Rice 54

Mug Peach Melba 55

Mug Buffalo Chicken Dip 56

Mug Lemon Bars 57

Mug Ratatouille 58

Mug Oatmeal Raisin Cookie 59

Mug Chicken Marsala 60

Mug Cherry Clafoutis 61

Mug Coconut Shrimp 62

Mug Black Forest Cake 63

Mug Caramel Apple Crisp 64

CONCLUSION 65

INTRODUCTION

Welcome to the world of culinary convenience, where flavor meets efficiency—Mug Meals! In this cookbook, we embark on a journey through the realm of quick and delectable recipes designed for the modern, fast-paced lifestyle. Picture this: a single mug, a handful of simple ingredients, and a microwave—that's all you need to whip up a delicious feast in minutes.

Mug meals are a culinary revolution, offering a time-saving solution for individuals with busy schedules, college students craving home-cooked flavors in their dorms, or anyone seeking a hassle-free approach to cooking. Whether you're a novice in the kitchen or a seasoned chef looking for a speedy alternative, mug meals are the perfect answer.

This cookbook is crafted for those who find themselves pressed for time, yet refuse to compromise on taste. Busy professionals, parents juggling multiple responsibilities, or students navigating the demands of academia—Mug Meals cater to all. The recipes featured within these pages range from savory to sweet, breakfast to dinner, and everything in between. Indulge in the culinary simplicity of creating personalized, portion-controlled dishes that burst with flavor and satisfy your cravings without the need for an extensive grocery list or complicated techniques.

Get ready to elevate your microwave game and revolutionize your approach to home-cooked meals—one mug at a time!

CHAPTER ONE

What are mug recipes?

Mug recipes, also known as mug meals or microwave mug recipes, are a trendy and convenient way to prepare quick, single-servings of various dishes using a microwave-safe mug. These recipes are designed for those who are short on time, have limited cooking equipment, or simply want a fast and easy way to satisfy their culinary cravings. Mug recipes span a wide range of culinary delights, from breakfast to dessert, and encompass a diverse array of flavors and ingredients.

Typically, mug recipes involve combining ingredients in a mug, stirring them together, and then microwaving the mixture for a short amount of time. The result is a quick, single-serving dish that minimizes preparation and cleanup. Some popular examples of mug recipes include mug cakes, mug omelets, mug brownies, and mug macaroni and cheese. These recipes often use simple pantry staples and are adaptable to personal tastes.

Mug recipes are not only time-efficient but also offer a great way to experiment with flavors and ingredients in a small-scale setting. They are particularly popular among individuals with busy schedules, college students in dorms, or anyone looking for a quick and easy cooking solution. The versatility and simplicity of mug recipes make them a fun and accessible way to enjoy homemade meals without the need for a full kitchen setup.

Tips for Making Nice Mug Meals

Creating delicious mug meals can be a rewarding and efficient way to enjoy quick, homemade dishes. Here are some tips to help you make the most of your mug meal experience:

1. Choose the Right Mug: Use a microwave-safe mug with enough capacity to accommodate the ingredients without overflowing during cooking. A larger mug also helps prevent spills and ensures even cooking.

2. Prep Ingredients Ahead of Time: Pre-measure your ingredients before starting the cooking process. This ensures a smoother and faster preparation, especially when you're working with limited time.

3. Mind the Ratios: Pay attention to the ratios of wet to dry ingredients. Achieving the right balance is crucial for the texture and taste of your mug meal. Too much or too little of certain ingredients can affect the outcome.

4. Mix Thoroughly: Ensure that all ingredients are well-mixed to avoid uneven cooking. Use a fork or a small whisk to blend the ingredients thoroughly, reaching the bottom and corners of the mug.

5. Consider Layering: Layer ingredients based on their cooking times. Place denser or longer-cooking ingredients at the bottom and quicker-cooking items on top to ensure even cooking throughout.

6. Don't Overcrowd: Avoid overloading the mug with ingredients. Leaving some space at the top allows for the mixture to expand without overflowing during cooking.

7. Watch Cooking Time: Microwave cooking times can vary, so start with the recommended time in the recipe and adjust as needed. Keep an eye on your mug meal to prevent overcooking, which can result in a dry or rubbery texture.

8. Experiment with Flavors: Don't be afraid to experiment with herbs, spices, and other seasonings to add flavor to your mug meals. Customize recipes to suit your taste preferences.

9. Add Toppings After Cooking: For certain recipes like mug cakes or desserts, consider adding toppings like whipped cream, chocolate chips, or nuts after the mug meal has cooked to enhance both presentation and taste.

10. Let It Rest: Allow your mug meal to rest for a minute or two after cooking. This helps the flavors to meld and allows the temperature to even out, preventing burns.

Remember that mug meals offer a great opportunity for creativity and personalization, so feel free to adapt recipes to suit your taste and dietary preferences. Happy mug cooking!

Materials Needed To Make Mug Meals

Making mug meals is a convenient and straightforward process, and you don't need a lot of fancy equipment. Here are the basic materials you'll need to get started:

1. Microwave-Safe Mug: Choose a mug that is labeled as microwave-safe. It should be able to withstand the heat generated during the cooking process. Ceramic or glass mugs are often good choices.

2. Measuring Utensils: Have measuring spoons and cups on hand to ensure accurate quantities of ingredients. This is especially important for maintaining the right balance of wet and dry ingredients.

3. Microwave: Obviously, a microwave is essential for cooking mug meals. Ensure that it's in good working condition and follow the recommended cooking times in your recipes.

4. Ingredients: Depending on the recipe, gather ingredients such as flour, sugar, eggs, milk, oil, spices, vegetables, and any other items specified in the recipe. Keep these items stocked in your pantry for quick and easy access.

5. Mixing Utensils: Use a fork, small whisk, or spoon for mixing ingredients in the mug. Make sure to reach the bottom and corners of the mug to ensure even mixing.

6. Cutting Board and Knife (if needed): Some mug meals may require chopping or slicing ingredients. Have a small cutting board and a knife on hand for these preparations.

7. Spoons or Forks: You'll need utensils for eating your mug meal once it's cooked. Choose the appropriate utensil based on the type of dish you're preparing.

8. Trivet or Hot Pad: After cooking, the mug will be hot. Use a trivet or hot pad to protect your hands and surfaces when handling the hot mug.

9. Optional Toppings: Depending on the recipe, you might want to have optional toppings like shredded cheese, herbs, sauces, or whipped cream to enhance the flavor of your mug meal.

10. Paper Towels or Napkins: Keep some paper towels or napkins handy for cleaning up any spills or messes during the preparation process.

CHAPTER TWO: MUG RECIPES

Classic Mug Brownie

Ingredients:

- 4 tablespoons all-purpose flour
- 4 tablespoons granulated sugar
- 2 tablespoons unsweetened cocoa powder
- 3 tablespoons vegetable oil
- 3 tablespoons water
- A pinch of salt
- A few drops of vanilla extract

Method:

1. In a microwave-safe mug, whisk together the flour, sugar, cocoa powder, and salt.

2. Add the vegetable oil, water, and vanilla extract to the mug. Stir until well combined.

3. Microwave on high for 1-2 minutes, depending on your microwave's wattage. The brownie should be set but still moist.

4. Let it cool for a minute before digging in. Optionally, top with whipped cream or a scoop of ice cream.

Average Preparation Time: 5 minutes

Nutritional Information: *(Approximate values per serving) - Calories: 300 - Fat: 15g - Carbohydrates: 40g - Protein: 3g*

Blueberry Muffin in a Mug

Ingredients:

- 4 tablespoons all-purpose flour
- 2 tablespoons granulated sugar
- 1/8 teaspoon baking powder
- 3 tablespoons milk
- 2 tablespoons vegetable oil
- 1/4 teaspoon vanilla extract
- A handful of fresh or frozen blueberries

Method:

1. In a microwave-safe mug, whisk together the flour, sugar, and baking powder.

2. Add the milk, vegetable oil, and vanilla extract. Stir until smooth.

3. Gently fold in the blueberries.

4. Microwave on high for 1-2 minutes until the muffin has risen and set.

5. Allow it to cool for a minute before eating.

Average Preparation Time: 5 minutes

Nutritional Information: (Approximate values per serving)

- *Calories: 320 - Fat: 16g - Carbohydrates: 42g*
- *Protein: 4g*

Loaded Baked Potato Mug

Ingredients:

- 1 large potato, peeled and diced
- 2 tablespoons shredded cheddar cheese
- 1 tablespoon sour cream
- 1 tablespoon chopped green onions
- Salt and pepper to taste

Method:

1. Place the diced potato in a microwave-safe mug. Add a splash of water and cover with a microwave-safe plate.

2. Microwave on high for 5-7 minutes until the potato is tender.

3. Drain any excess water and mash the potato with a fork.

4. Stir in the cheese, sour cream, green onions, salt, and pepper.

5. Microwave for an additional 1-2 minutes until the cheese is melted.

6. Allow to cool off slightly before serving.

Average Preparation Time: 10 minutes

Nutritional Information: (Approximate values per serving)

- Calories: 250   - Fat: 8g

- Carbohydrates: 38gm - Protein: 6g

Spinach and Feta Mug Omelette

Ingredients:

- 2 eggs
- 2 tablespoons milk
- 2 tablespoons fresh spinach, chopped
- 2 tablespoons feta cheese, crumbled
- Salt and pepper to taste

Method:

1. In a mug, whisk together the eggs and milk.

2. Stir in the chopped spinach, feta cheese, salt, and pepper.

3. Microwave on high for 1-2 minutes, pausing to stir halfway through, until the eggs are set.

4. Let it cool off for a minute before eating.

Average Preparation Time: 5 minutes

Nutritional Information: (Approximate values per serving)

- *Calories: 220*
- *Fat: 15g*
- *Carbohydrates: 3g*
- *Protein: 18g*

Mug Pizza

Ingredients:

- 4 tablespoons all-purpose flour
- 1/8 teaspoon baking powder
- 1/16 teaspoon baking soda
- 1/8 teaspoon salt
- 3 tablespoons milk
- 1 tablespoon olive oil
- 1 tablespoon pizza sauce
- 2 tablespoons shredded mozzarella cheese
- Your favorite pizza toppings (e.g., pepperoni, olives, bell peppers)

Method:

1. In a mug, whisk together the flour, baking powder, baking soda, and salt.

2. Add the milk and olive oil. Stir until smooth.

3. Spoon pizza sauce over the batter, spreading it out evenly.

4. Sprinkle cheese and your desired toppings on top.

5. Microwave on high for 1-2 minutes until the pizza is cooked through.

6. Allow it to cool for a minute before slicing.

Average Preparation Time: 7 minutes

Nutritional Information: (Approximate values per serving) - *Calories: 400 - Fat: 20g - Carbohydrates: 40g - Protein: 15g*

Chocolate Chip Cookie in a Mug

Ingredients:

- 1 tablespoon unsalted butter
- 1 tablespoon granulated sugar
- 1 tablespoon brown sugar
- 1/8 teaspoon vanilla extract
- A pinch of salt
- 1 egg yolk
- 3 tablespoons all-purpose flour
- 2 tablespoons chocolate chips

Method:

1. In a mug, melt the butter in the microwave.

2. Stir in the granulated sugar, brown sugar, vanilla extract, and a pinch of salt.

3. Add the egg yolk and mix very well.

4. Stir in the flour until combined, then fold in the chocolate chips.

5. Microwave on high for 40-60 seconds until the cookie is set but still soft in the middle.

6. Allow it to cool for a minute before enjoying.

Average Preparation Time: 5 minutes

Nutritional Information: (Approximate values per serving) - *Calories: 350 - Fat: 18g - Carbohydrates: 45g - Protein: 5g*

Mug Banana Bread

Ingredients:

- 1 ripe banana, mashed
- 2 tablespoons melted butter
- 3 tablespoons brown sugar
- 1/8 teaspoon vanilla extract
- A pinch of salt
- 1/4 teaspoon baking powder
- 1/4 teaspoon cinnamon
- 1/3 cup all-purpose flour
- Optional: chopped nuts or chocolate chips

Method:

1. In a mug, mix the mashed banana, melted butter, brown sugar, and vanilla extract.

2. Add the salt, baking powder, cinnamon, and flour. Stir until just combined.

3. Fold in nuts or chocolate chips if desired.

4. Microwave on high for 2-3 minutes until the bread is set and a toothpick comes out clean.

5. Let it cool for a minute before slicing.

Average Preparation Time: 7 minutes

Nutritional Information: (Approximate values per serving) - *Calories: 300 - Fat: 12g - Carbohydrates: 45g*

- *Protein: 4g*

Mug Egg Fried Rice

Ingredients:

- 1 cup cooked rice
- 1 egg
- 1 tablespoon soy sauce
- 1 tablespoon chopped green onions
- 1/4 cup frozen peas and carrots (thawed)
- 1 tablespoon vegetable oil

Method:

1. In a mug, heat the vegetable oil in the microwave for 30 seconds.

2. Add the cooked rice, egg, soy sauce, green onions, and thawed peas and carrots. Stir well.

3. Microwave on high for 2-3 minutes, stirring halfway through, until the egg is cooked and the rice is heated through.

4. Allow it to cool for a minute before eating.

Average Preparation Time: 5 minutes

Nutritional Information: (Approximate values per serving)

- Calories: 350   - Fat: 14g

- Carbohydrates: 45g - Protein: 10g

Peanut Butter Mug Cake

Ingredients:

- 4 tablespoons all-purpose flour
- 2 tablespoons granulated sugar
- 1/8 teaspoon baking powder
- 3 tablespoons milk
- 2 tablespoons peanut butter
- A few drops of vanilla extract

Method:

1. In a mug, whisk together the flour, sugar, and baking powder.

2. Add the milk, peanut butter, and vanilla extract. Stir until smooth.

3. Microwave on high for 1-2 minutes until the cake is set.

4. Let it cool for a minute before digging in.

Average Preparation Time: 5 minutes

Nutritional Information: (Approximate values per serving)

- Calories: 400
- Fat: 20g
- Carbohydrates: 45g
- Protein: 10g

Cheesy Broccoli Mug Casserole

Ingredients:

- 1 cup broccoli florets, steamed
- 1/4 cup shredded cheddar cheese
- 2 tablespoons milk
- 1 tablespoon cream cheese
- 2 tablespoons breadcrumbs
- Salt and pepper to taste

Method:

1. In a mug, combine the steamed broccoli, cheddar cheese, milk, and cream cheese. Mix well.

2. Season with salt and pepper to taste.

3. Top the mixture with breadcrumbs.

4. Microwave on high for 2-3 minutes until the casserole is heated through and the cheese is melted.

5. Allow it to cool for a minute before serving.

Average Preparation Time: 7 minutes

Nutritional Information: (Approximate values per serving)

- *Calories: 250*
- *Fat: 15g*
- *Carbohydrates: 20g*
- *Protein: 10g*

Mug Pumpkin Pie

Ingredients:

- 3 tablespoons pumpkin puree
- 2 tablespoons sweetened condensed milk
- 1 egg yolk
- 1/4 teaspoon pumpkin pie spice
- Graham cracker crumbs (for crust)

Method:

1. In a mug, mix the pumpkin puree, sweetened condensed milk, egg yolk, and pumpkin pie spice until well combined.

2. Sprinkle graham cracker crumbs over the mixture to form a crust.

3. Microwave on high for 2-3 minutes until the pie is set.

4. Allow it to cool before serving.

Average Preparation Time: 5 minutes

Nutritional Information: (Approximate values per serving)

- Calories: 200
- Fat: 8g
- Carbohydrates: 30g
- Protein: 5g

Caprese Mug Scramble

Ingredients:

- 2 eggs
- 2 tablespoons milk
- 2 tablespoons cherry tomatoes, halved
- 2 tablespoons fresh mozzarella, diced
- 1 tablespoon fresh basil, chopped
- Salt and pepper to taste
- 1 teaspoon olive oil

Method:

1. In a mug, whisk together the eggs and milk.

2. Add cherry tomatoes, mozzarella, basil, salt, and pepper. Mix well.

3. Drizzle olive oil over the mixture.

4. Microwave on high for 1-2 minutes, stirring halfway through, until the eggs are set.

5. Allow it to cool for a minute before serving.

Average Preparation Time: 5 minutes

Nutritional Information: (Approximate values per serving)

- Calories: 250
- Fat: 18g
- Carbohydrates: 5g
- Protein: 15g

S'mores Mug Cake:

Ingredients:

- 4 tablespoons graham cracker crumbs
- 2 tablespoons unsweetened cocoa powder
- 2 tablespoons granulated sugar
- 1/8 teaspoon baking powder
- 3 tablespoons milk
- 2 tablespoons vegetable oil
- 1/4 teaspoon vanilla extract
- 2 tablespoons mini marshmallows
- 1 tablespoon chocolate chips

Method:

1. In a mug, whisk together graham cracker crumbs, cocoa powder, sugar, and baking powder.

2. Add milk, vegetable oil, and vanilla extract. Stir until smooth.

3. Sprinkle mini marshmallows and chocolate chips on top.

4. Microwave on high for 1-2 minutes until the cake is set and the marshmallows are puffed.

5. Allow it to cool for a minute before indulging.

Average Preparation Time: 5 minutes

Nutritional Information: (Approximate values per serving)

- *Calories: 350 - Fat: 20g*
- *Carbohydrates: 45g - Protein: 5g*

Cinnamon Roll in a Mug

Ingredients:

- 4 tablespoons all-purpose flour
- 1/2 teaspoon baking powder
- 2 tablespoons milk
- 1 tablespoon melted butter
- 1 tablespoon brown sugar
- 1/2 teaspoon ground cinnamon
- Cream cheese frosting (optional)

Method:

1. In a mug, whisk together the flour and baking powder.

2. Add milk and melted butter. Mix until smooth.

3. In a separate small bowl, combine brown sugar and cinnamon.

4. Sprinkle the cinnamon sugar mixture over the batter in the mug.

5. Microwave on high for 1-2 minutes until the cinnamon roll is cooked through.

6. Drizzle with cream cheese frosting if desired.

7. Allow it to cool for a minute before enjoying.

Average Preparation Time: 5 minutes

Nutritional Information: (Approximate values per serving)

- Calories: 300 - Fat: 15g
- Carbohydrates: 40g - Protein: 4g

Chicken Alfredo Mug Pasta

Ingredients:

- 1/2 cup cooked pasta
- 1/4 cup cooked chicken, shredded
- 2 tablespoons Alfredo sauce
- 2 tablespoons grated Parmesan cheese
- Salt and pepper to taste
- Chopped parsley for garnish

Method:

1. In a mug, combine cooked pasta, shredded chicken, Alfredo sauce, Parmesan cheese, salt, and pepper.

2. Mix well to coat the pasta and chicken evenly.

3. Microwave on high for 1-2 minutes until heated through.

4. Garnish with chopped parsley before serving.

Average Preparation Time: 5 minutes

Nutritional Information: (Approximate values per serving)

- Calories: 400
- Fat: 20g
- Carbohydrates: 30g
- Protein: 25g

Mug Lemon Poppy Seed Muffin

Ingredients:

- 4 tablespoons all-purpose flour
- 2 tablespoons granulated sugar
- 1/4 teaspoon baking powder
- 2 tablespoons milk
- 1/2 tablespoon vegetable oil
- 1/2 tablespoon lemon juice
- 1/2 teaspoon lemon zest
- 1/2 teaspoon poppy seeds

Method:

1. In a mug, whisk together the flour, sugar, and baking powder.

2. Add milk, vegetable oil, lemon juice, lemon zest, and poppy seeds. Stir until smooth.

3. Microwave on high for 1-2 minutes until the muffin is cooked through.

4. Allow it to cool for a minute before enjoying.

Average Preparation Time: 5 minutes

Nutritional Information: (Approximate values per serving)

- *Calories: 250*
- *Fat: 10g*
- *Carbohydrates: 35g*
- *Protein: 4g*

Mac and Cheese in a Mug

Ingredients:

- 1/2 cup elbow macaroni, cooked
- 1/4 cup shredded cheddar cheese
- 2 tablespoons milk
- 1/2 tablespoon butter
- 1/4 teaspoon mustard
- Salt and pepper to taste

Method:

1. In a mug, combine cooked macaroni, shredded cheddar cheese, milk, butter, mustard, salt, and pepper.

2. Stir well to melt the cheese and coat the macaroni.

3. Microwave on high for 1-2 minutes until the cheese is melted and the macaroni is heated through.

4. Allow it to cool for a minute before serving.

Average Preparation Time: 5 minutes

Nutritional Information: (Approximate values per serving)

- *Calories: 300*
- *Fat: 15g*
- *Carbohydrates: 30g*
- *Protein: 10g*

Mug Chicken Pot Pie

Ingredients:

- 1/2 cup cooked chicken, shredded
- 1/4 cup frozen mixed vegetables (peas, carrots, corn)
- 2 tablespoons cream of chicken soup
- 1/4 cup milk
- Salt and pepper to taste
- Biscuit dough for topping

Method:

1. In a mug, mix shredded chicken, frozen mixed vegetables, cream of chicken soup, milk, salt, and pepper.

2. Top the mixture with a small piece of biscuit dough.

3. Microwave on high for 2-3 minutes until the filling is hot and the biscuit is cooked through.

4. Allow it to cool for a minute before serving.

Average Preparation Time: 7 minutes

Nutritional Information: (Approximate values per serving)

- *Calories: 350*
- *Fat: 15g*
- *Carbohydrates: 35g*
- *Protein: 20g*

Raspberry Mug Pancake

Ingredients:

- 4 tablespoons all-purpose flour
- 1 tablespoon granulated sugar
- 1/4 teaspoon baking powder
- 3 tablespoons milk
- 1/2 tablespoon melted butter
- 1/4 teaspoon vanilla extract
- Fresh raspberries for topping
- Maple syrup for serving

Method:

1. In a mug, whisk together the flour, sugar, and baking powder.

2. Add milk, melted butter, and vanilla extract. Stir until smooth.

3. Microwave on high for 1-2 minutes until the pancake is cooked through.

4. Top with fresh raspberries and drizzle with maple syrup before serving.

Average Preparation Time: 5 minutes

Nutritional Information: (Approximate values per serving)

- *Calories: 300 - Fat: 12g - Carbohydrates: 40g*
- *Protein: 5g*

Mug Tuna Noodle Casserole

Ingredients:

- 1/2 cup cooked egg noodles
- 1/4 cup canned tuna, drained
- 2 tablespoons frozen peas
- 2 tablespoons mayonnaise
- 2 tablespoons milk
- 2 tablespoons shredded cheddar cheese
- Salt and pepper to taste
- Crushed potato chips for topping (optional)

Method:

1. In a mug, combine cooked egg noodles, canned tuna, frozen peas, mayonnaise, milk, shredded cheddar cheese, salt, and pepper.

2. Mix well and top with crushed potato chips if desired.

3. Microwave on high for 2-3 minutes until the casserole is heated through.

4. Allow it to cool for a minute before serving.

Average Preparation Time: 7 minutes

Nutritional Information: (Approximate values per serving)

- *Calories: 350 - Fat: 20g - Carbohydrates: 25g*
- *Protein: 15g*

Mug Coffee Cake

Ingredients:

- 4 tablespoons all-purpose flour
- 2 tablespoons brown sugar
- 1/8 teaspoon baking powder
- 2 tablespoons unsalted butter, softened
- 2 tablespoons milk
- 1/4 teaspoon vanilla extract
- Cinnamon-sugar mixture for topping

Method:

1. In a mug, mix the flour, brown sugar, and baking powder.

2. Add the softened butter, milk, and vanilla extract. Stir until smooth.

3. Sprinkle a layer of the cinnamon-sugar mixture on top.

4. Microwave on high for 1-2 minutes until the cake is set.

5. Allow it to cool for a minute before enjoying.

Average Preparation Time: 5 minutes

Nutritional Information: (Approximate values per serving)

- *Calories: 300 - Fat: 15g*
- *Carbohydrates: 40g - Protein: 3g*

Caprese Mug Pasta

Ingredients:

- 1/2 cup cooked pasta
- 2 tablespoons cherry tomatoes, halved
- 2 tablespoons fresh mozzarella, diced
- 1 tablespoon fresh basil, chopped
- 1 tablespoon olive oil
- Salt and pepper to taste

Method:

1. In a mug, combine cooked pasta, cherry tomatoes, fresh mozzarella, basil, olive oil, salt, and pepper.

2. Toss gently until ingredients are well mixed.

3. Microwave on high for 1-2 minutes until the pasta is heated through and the cheese is slightly melted.

4. Allow it to cool for a minute before serving.

Average Preparation Time: 5 minutes

Nutritional Information: (Approximate values per serving)

- *Calories: 300*
- *Fat: 15g*
- *Carbohydrates: 35g*
- *Protein: 10g*

Mug Taco Soup

Ingredients:

- 1/4 cup cooked ground beef or turkey
- 1/4 cup canned black beans, drained and rinsed
- 2 tablespoons corn kernels
- 2 tablespoons diced tomatoes
- 2 tablespoons salsa
- 1/4 cup beef or vegetable broth
- 1/2 teaspoon taco seasoning
- Optional toppings: shredded cheese, sour cream, chopped green onions

Method:

1. In a mug, combine cooked ground beef or turkey, black beans, corn, diced tomatoes, salsa, beef or vegetable broth, and taco seasoning.

2. Mix well and microwave on high for 2-3 minutes until the soup is heated through.

3. Top with shredded cheese, sour cream, and chopped green onions if desired.

4. Allow it to cool for a minute before enjoying.

Average Preparation Time: 7 minutes

Nutritional Information: (Approximate values per serving)

- *Calories: 300 - Fat: 15g - Carbohydrates: 30g*
- *Protein: 15g*

Mug Apple Crisp

Ingredients:

- 1 small apple, peeled and diced
- 1/4 teaspoon ground cinnamon
- 1/2 tablespoon granulated sugar
- 2 tablespoons old-fashioned oats
- 1 tablespoon flour
- 1 tablespoon unsalted butter, melted
- Vanilla ice cream for serving (optional)

Method:

1. In a mug, toss the diced apple with ground cinnamon and granulated sugar.

2. In a separate bowl, mix old-fashioned oats, flour, and melted butter.

3. Sprinkle the oat mixture over the apples in the mug.

4. Microwave on high for 2-3 minutes until the apples are tender.

5. Allow it to cool for a minute before serving, optionally topping with vanilla ice cream.

Average Preparation Time: 7 minutes

Nutritional Information: (Approximate values per serving)
- Calories: 250   - Fat: 10g
- Carbohydrates: 40g - Protein: 2g

Mug Ramen

Ingredients:

- 1 packet of instant ramen noodles (discard seasoning if desired)
- 2 cups water
- 1/2 cup mixed vegetables (carrots, peas, corn)
- 1 tablespoon soy sauce
- 1/2 tablespoon sesame oil
- Green onions and sesame seeds for garnish

Method:

1. Break the ramen noodles into the mug and add mixed vegetables.

2. Pour 2 cups of water into the mug.

3. Microwave on high for 3-4 minutes or until noodles are cooked.

4. Drain excess water, leaving about 1-2 tablespoons in the mug.

5. Add soy sauce and sesame oil. Stir well.

6. Garnish with green onions and sesame seeds before serving.

Average Preparation Time: 7 minutes

Nutritional Information: (Approximate values per serving)

- - Calories: 350   - Fat: 10g
- - Carbohydrates: 50g   - Protein: 10g

Mug Quiche Lorraine

Ingredients:

- 1 egg
- 2 tablespoons milk
- 1 tablespoon heavy cream
- 2 tablespoons cooked bacon, crumbled
- 1 tablespoon grated Gruyere or Swiss cheese
- Salt and pepper to taste
- Chopped chives for garnish

Method:

1. In a mug, whisk together the egg, milk, and heavy cream.

2. Add crumbled bacon, grated cheese, salt, and pepper. Mix well.

3. Microwave on high for 2-3 minutes until the quiche is set.

4. Garnish with chopped chives before serving.

Average Preparation Time: 5 minutes

Nutritional Information: (Approximate values per serving)

- Calories: 300
- Fat: 20g
- Carbohydrates: 5g
- Protein: 15g

Red Velvet Mug Cake

Ingredients:

- 4 tablespoons all-purpose flour
- 2 tablespoons granulated sugar
- 1/8 teaspoon baking powder
- 2 tablespoons buttermilk
- 1 tablespoon vegetable oil
- 1/4 teaspoon vanilla extract
- 1/4 teaspoon red food coloring
- Cream cheese frosting for topping (optional)

Method:

1. In a mug, whisk together the flour, sugar, and baking powder.

2. Add your buttermilk, vegetable oil, vanilla extract, and red food coloring. Stir until smooth.

3. Microwave on high for 1-2 minutes until the cake is set.

4. Allow it to cool for a minute before topping with cream cheese frosting if desired.

Average Preparation Time: 5 minutes

Nutritional Information: (Approximate values per serving)

- Calories: 350
- Fat: 18g
- Carbohydrates: 45g
- Protein: 4g

Mug Vegetable Stir-Fry

Ingredients:

- 1/2 cup mixed vegetables (broccoli, bell peppers, carrots)
- 1 tablespoon soy sauce
- 1/2 tablespoon sesame oil
- 1/2 tablespoon honey
- 1/2 tablespoon olive oil
- 1/2 tablespoon ginger, minced
- 1/2 tablespoon garlic, minced
- Sesame seeds for garnish

Method:

1. In a mug, combine mixed vegetables, soy sauce, sesame oil, honey, olive oil, minced ginger, and minced garlic.

2. Stir well and microwave on high for 2-3 minutes until the vegetables are cooked but still crisp.

3. Garnish with sesame seeds before serving.

Average Preparation Time: 5 minutes

Nutritional Information: (Approximate values per serving)

- *Calories: 150*
- *Fat: 8g*
- *Carbohydrates: 20g*
- *Protein: 2g*

Mug Cheesecake

Ingredients:

- 2 tablespoons cream cheese, softened
- 2 tablespoons granulated sugar
- 2 tablespoons sour cream
- 1/4 teaspoon vanilla extract
- 1 egg
- Graham cracker crumbs for crust (optional)
- Fruit or berry topping (optional)

Method:

1. In a mug, beat together cream cheese, sugar, sour cream, vanilla extract, and egg until smooth.

2. Optionally, sprinkle a layer of graham cracker crumbs on the bottom for a crust.

3. Microwave on high for 2-3 minutes until the cheesecake is set.

4. Allow it to cool for a minute before adding fruit or berry topping if desired.

Average Preparation Time: 5 minutes

Nutritional Information: (Approximate values per serving)

- *Calories: 350*
- *Fat: 25g*
- *Carbohydrates: 25g*
- *Protein: 6g*

Mug Mediterranean Couscous

Ingredients:

- 1/4 cup couscous, cooked
- 2 tablespoons cherry tomatoes, halved
- 1 tablespoon cucumber, diced
- 1 tablespoon feta cheese, crumbled
- 1 tablespoon Kalamata olives, sliced
- 1 tablespoon olive oil
- 1/2 tablespoon lemon juice
- Fresh parsley for garnish

Method:

1. In a mug, combine cooked couscous, cherry tomatoes, cucumber, feta cheese, and Kalamata olives.

2. Drizzle with olive oil and lemon juice. Mix well.

3. Microwave on high for 1-2 minutes until the couscous is heated through.

4. Garnish with fresh parsley before serving.

Average Preparation Time: 5 minutes

Nutritional Information: (Approximate values per serving)

- *Calories: 300*
- *Fat: 15g*
- *Carbohydrates: 35g*
- *Protein: 8g*

Mug Key Lime Pie

Ingredients:

- 2 tablespoons graham cracker crumbs
- 1 tablespoon unsalted butter, melted
- 2 tablespoons sweetened condensed milk
- 1 tablespoon key lime juice
- Whipped cream for topping

Method:

1. In a mug, combine graham cracker crumbs and melted butter for the crust.

2. Press the crust mixture into the bottom of the mug.

3. In a separate bowl, mix sweetened condensed milk and key lime juice.

4. Pour the key lime mixture over the crust in the mug.

5. Microwave on high for 1-2 minutes until set.

6. Allow it to cool before topping with whipped cream.

Average Preparation Time: 5 minutes

Nutritional Information: (Approximate values per serving)

- *Calories: 250*
- *Fat: 15g*
- *Carbohydrates: 25g*
- *Protein: 4g*

Mug Shrimp Scampi

Ingredients:

- 1/2 cup cooked shrimp, peeled and deveined
- 2 tablespoons unsalted butter
- 1 tablespoon minced garlic
- 1 tablespoon white wine (optional)
- 1 tablespoon fresh lemon juice
- 1/2 tablespoon chopped parsley
- Salt and pepper to taste
- Red pepper flakes for a kick (optional)

Method:

1. In a mug, melt the butter in the microwave.

2. Add the minced garlic and cook for 30 seconds.

3. Stir in cooked shrimp, white wine (if using), lemon juice, chopped parsley, salt, pepper, and red pepper flakes (if desired).

4. Microwave on high for 1-2 minutes until the shrimp are heated through.

5. Allow it to cool for a minute before serving.

Average Preparation Time: 5 minutes

Nutritional Information: (Approximate values per serving)
- Calories: 300
- Fat: 20g
- Carbohydrates: 5g
- Protein: 20g

Mug French Toast

Ingredients:

- 1 slice of bread, cubed
- 1 egg
- 2 tablespoons milk
- 1/2 tablespoon maple syrup
- 1/4 teaspoon ground cinnamon
- A pinch of salt
- Powdered sugar for dusting (optional)

Method:

1. In a mug, whisk together egg, milk, maple syrup, ground cinnamon, and a pinch of salt.

2. Add cubed bread to the egg mixture, ensuring all pieces are coated.

3. Microwave on high for 1-2 minutes until the French toast is set.

4. Dust with powdered sugar if desired before serving.

Average Preparation Time: 5 minutes

Nutritional Information: (Approximate values per serving)

- Calories: 250
- Fat: 10g
- Carbohydrates: 30g
- Protein: 10g

Mug Chicken Enchilada

Ingredients:

- 1/2 cup cooked chicken, shredded
- 2 tablespoons black beans, drained and rinsed
- 2 tablespoons corn kernels
- 2 tablespoons enchilada sauce
- 1 tablespoon shredded cheddar cheese
- 1 tablespoon chopped cilantro
- Tortilla chips for dipping (optional)

Method:

1. In a mug, combine shredded chicken, black beans, corn, and enchilada sauce.

2. Microwave on high for 2-3 minutes until the mixture is heated through.

3. Top with shredded cheddar cheese and microwave for an additional 30 seconds until melted.

4. Garnish with chopped cilantro and serve with tortilla chips if desired.

Average Preparation Time: 5 minutes

Nutritional Information: (Approximate values per serving)

- *Calories: 300*
- *Fat: 15g*
- *Carbohydrates: 20g*
- *Protein: 20g*

Mug Pesto Pasta

Ingredients:

- 1/2 cup cooked pasta
- 2 tablespoons basil pesto
- 1 tablespoon grated Parmesan cheese
- Cherry tomatoes for garnish
- Pine nuts for garnish (optional)

Method:

1. In a mug, mix cooked pasta with basil pesto until well coated.

2. Sprinkle grated Parmesan cheese on top.

3. Microwave on high for 1-2 minutes until the pasta is heated through.

4. Garnish with cherry tomatoes and pine nuts if desired before serving.

Average Preparation Time: 5 minutes

Nutritional Information: (Approximate values per serving)

- *Calories: 350*
- *Fat: 20g*
- *Carbohydrates: 30g*
- *Protein: 10g*

Mug Chocolate Pudding

Ingredients:

- 2 tablespoons sugar
- 1 tablespoon unsweetened cocoa powder
- 2 tablespoons cornstarch
- A pinch of salt
- 3/4 cup milk
- 1/2 teaspoon vanilla extract

Method:

1. In a mug, whisk together sugar, cocoa powder, cornstarch, and salt.

2. Gradually add milk, whisking constantly to avoid lumps.

3. Microwave on high for 2-3 minutes, stirring every 30 seconds, until the pudding thickens.

4. Stir in vanilla extract and let it cool for a few minutes before serving.

Average Preparation Time: 5 minutes

Nutritional Information: (Approximate values per serving)

- Calories: 200
- Fat: 5g
- Carbohydrates: 35g
- Protein: 5g

Mug Margherita Pizza

Ingredients:

- 1 small tortilla
- 2 tablespoons pizza sauce
- 2 tablespoons shredded mozzarella cheese
- Fresh basil leaves for topping
- Cherry tomatoes for topping

Method:

1. Place the tortilla in a mug to create a crust.

2. Spread pizza sauce over the tortilla.

3. Sprinkle shredded mozzarella cheese on top.

4. Add fresh basil leaves and cherry tomatoes as toppings.

5. Microwave on high for 1-2 minutes until the cheese is melted.

6. Allow it to cool for a minute before slicing.

Average Preparation Time: 5 minutes

Nutritional Information: (Approximate values per serving)

- Calories: 250
- Fat: 10g
- Carbohydrates: 30g
- Protein: 10g

Mug Sweet and Sour Chicken

Ingredients:

- 1/2 cup cooked chicken, diced
- 2 tablespoons pineapple chunks
- 1 tablespoon ketchup
- 1 tablespoon rice vinegar
- 1 tablespoon brown sugar
- 1 tablespoon soy sauce
- 1/2 tablespoon cornstarch
- Bell peppers and onions for additional vegetables

Method:

1. In a mug, combine cooked chicken, pineapple chunks, ketchup, rice vinegar, brown sugar, soy sauce, and cornstarch.

2. Add bell peppers and onions if desired.

3. Microwave on high for 2-3 minutes until the chicken is heated through and the sauce thickens.

4. Allow it to cool for a minute before serving.

Average Preparation Time: 7 minutes

Nutritional Information: (Approximate values per serving)

- Calories: 300
- Fat: 10g
- Carbohydrates: 30g
- Protein: 20g

Mug Blueberry Cobbler

Ingredients:

- 1/2 cup fresh or frozen blueberries
- 2 tablespoons granulated sugar
- 2 tablespoons all-purpose flour
- 1/4 teaspoon baking powder
- A pinch of salt
- 2 tablespoons milk
- 1/2 tablespoon melted butter

Method:

1. In a mug, mix blueberries with sugar, flour, baking powder, and a pinch of salt.

2. Add milk and melted butter. Stir until well combined.

3. Microwave on high for 2-3 minutes until the cobbler is set.

4. Allow it to cool for a minute before serving.

Average Preparation Time: 5 minutes

Nutritional Information: (Approximate values per serving)

- Calories: 250
- Fat: 8g
- Carbohydrates: 45g
- Protein: 2g

Mug Chicken and Rice

Ingredients:

- 1/2 cup cooked chicken, diced
- 1/4 cup cooked rice
- 2 tablespoons frozen mixed vegetables (peas, carrots, corn)
- 2 tablespoons chicken broth
- 1 tablespoon cream of mushroom soup
- Salt and pepper to taste

Method:

1. In a mug, combine cooked chicken, cooked rice, frozen mixed vegetables, chicken broth, and cream of mushroom soup.

2. Mix well and season with salt and pepper to taste.

3. Microwave on high for 2-3 minutes until the mixture is heated through.

4. Allow it to cool off for a minute before serving.

Average Preparation Time: 7 minutes

Nutritional Information: (Approximate values per serving)

- Calories: 350
- Fat: 15g
- Carbohydrates: 30g
- Protein: 20g

Mug Peach Melba

Ingredients:

- 1/2 cup sliced peaches (fresh or canned)
- 2 tablespoons raspberry sauce
- Vanilla ice cream for topping

Method:

1. In a mug, layer sliced peaches.

2. Pour raspberry sauce over the peaches.

3. Microwave on high for 1-2 minutes until the peaches are warm.

4. Top with vanilla ice cream before serving.

Average Preparation Time: 5 minutes

Nutritional Information: (Approximate values per serving)

- Calories: 150
- Fat: 2g
- Carbohydrates: 35g
- Protein: 1g

Mug Buffalo Chicken Dip

Ingredients:

- 1/2 cup cooked chicken, shredded
- 2 tablespoons cream cheese
- 2 tablespoons shredded cheddar cheese
- 1 tablespoon buffalo sauce
- 1 tablespoon ranch dressing
- Chopped green onions for garnish
- Tortilla chips for dipping

Method:

1. In a mug, mix shredded chicken, cream cheese, cheddar cheese, buffalo sauce, and ranch dressing.

2. Microwave on high for 2-3 minutes until the dip is hot and bubbly.

3. Garnish with chopped green onions.

4. Serve with tortilla chips for dipping.

Average Preparation Time: 5 minutes

Nutritional Information: (Approximate values per serving)

- Calories: 300
- Fat: 20g
- Carbohydrates: 5g
- Protein: 20g

Mug Lemon Bars

Ingredients:

- 4 tablespoons all-purpose flour
- 2 tablespoons granulated sugar
- 1/8 teaspoon baking powder
- 2 tablespoons lemon juice
- 1 teaspoon lemon zest
- 1 egg
- Powdered sugar for dusting

Method:

1. In a mug, whisk together flour, sugar, and baking powder.

2. Add lemon juice, lemon zest, and egg. Stir until smooth.

3. Microwave on high for 1-2 minutes until the bars are set.

4. Dust with powdered sugar before serving.

Average Preparation Time: 5 minutes

Nutritional Information: (Approximate values per serving)

- Calories: 250
- Fat: 5g
- Carbohydrates: 45g
- Protein: 5g

Mug Ratatouille

Ingredients:

- 1/2 cup eggplant, diced
- 1/2 cup zucchini, diced
- 1/4 cup bell peppers, diced
- 2 tablespoons tomato sauce
- 1 tablespoon olive oil
- 1/2 teaspoon dried herbs (thyme, rosemary, oregano)
- Salt and pepper to taste

Method:

1. In a mug, combine diced eggplant, zucchini, bell peppers, tomato sauce, olive oil, dried herbs, salt, and pepper.

2. Microwave on high for 3-4 minutes until the vegetables are tender.

3. Allow it to cool for a minute before serving.

Average Preparation Time: 7 minutes

Nutritional Information: (Approximate values per serving)

- Calories: 150
- Fat: 10g
- Carbohydrates: 15g
- Protein: 2g

Mug Oatmeal Raisin Cookie

Ingredients:

- 3 tablespoons rolled oats
- 2 tablespoons all-purpose flour
- 1/4 teaspoon baking powder
- 2 tablespoons unsalted butter, melted
- 2 tablespoons brown sugar
- 1/2 teaspoon vanilla extract
- 1 tablespoon raisins

Method:

1. In a mug, mix rolled oats, flour, baking powder, melted butter, brown sugar, vanilla extract, and raisins.

2. Microwave on high for 1-2 minutes until the cookie is set.

3. Allow it to cool for a minute before enjoying.

Average Preparation Time: 5 minutes

Nutritional Information: (Approximate values per serving)

- Calories: 300
- Fat: 15g
- Carbohydrates: 40g
- Protein: 3g

Mug Chicken Marsala

Ingredients:

- 1/2 cup cooked chicken, sliced
- 2 tablespoons Marsala wine
- 2 tablespoons chicken broth
- 1 tablespoon heavy cream
- 1 tablespoon unsalted butter
- 1/2 tablespoon flour
- Salt and pepper to taste
- Fresh parsley for garnish

Method:

1. In a mug, combine sliced chicken, Marsala wine, chicken broth, heavy cream, unsalted butter, flour, salt, and pepper.

2. Microwave on high for 2-3 minutes until the sauce thickens and the chicken is heated through.

3. Garnish with fresh parsley before serving.

Average Preparation Time: 5 minutes

Nutritional Information: (Approximate values per serving)

- Calories: 400
- Fat: 25g
- Carbohydrates: 5g
- Protein: 20g

Mug Cherry Clafoutis

Ingredients:

- 1/2 cup fresh or canned cherries, pitted
- 2 tablespoons all-purpose flour
- 1 tablespoon granulated sugar
- 2 tablespoons milk
- 1/2 teaspoon vanilla extract
- Powdered sugar for dusting

Method:

1. In a mug, place cherries.

2. In a bowl, whisk together flour, sugar, milk, and vanilla extract.

3. Pour the batter over the cherries in the mug.

4. Microwave on high for 2-3 minutes until the clafoutis is set.

5. Dust with powdered sugar before serving.

Average Preparation Time: 5 minutes

Nutritional Information: (Approximate values per serving)

- Calories: 250
- Fat: 2g
- Carbohydrates: 55g
- Protein: 2g

Mug Coconut Shrimp

Ingredients:

- 1/2 cup large shrimp, peeled and deveined
- 2 tablespoons shredded coconut
- 1 tablespoon panko breadcrumbs
- 1/2 tablespoon coconut oil, melted
- 1/2 tablespoon lime juice
- Salt and pepper to taste
- Sweet chili sauce for dipping

Method:

1. In a mug, combine shrimp, shredded coconut, panko breadcrumbs, melted coconut oil, lime juice, salt, and pepper.

2. Microwave on high for 2-3 minutes until the shrimp are cooked through and coconut is golden.

3. Serve with sweet chili sauce for dipping.

Average Preparation Time: 7 minutes

Nutritional Information: (Approximate values per serving)

- *Calories: 250*
- *Fat: 15g*
- *Carbohydrates:15g*
- *Protein: 15g*

Mug Black Forest Cake

Ingredients:

- 4 tablespoons all-purpose flour
- 2 tablespoons granulated sugar
- 1/8 teaspoon baking powder
- 2 tablespoons cocoa powder
- 3 tablespoons milk
- 2 tablespoons vegetable oil
- 1/4 teaspoon vanilla extract
- 2 tablespoons canned cherries, pitted and halved
- Whipped cream for topping

Method:

1. In a mug, whisk together flour, sugar, baking powder, and cocoa powder.

2. Add milk, vegetable oil, and vanilla extract. Stir until smooth.

3. Drop the cherry halves into the batter.

4. Microwave on high for 1-2 minutes until the cake is set.

5. Top with whipped cream before serving.

Average Preparation Time: 5 minutes

Nutritional Information: (Approximate values per serving)

- *Calories: 350*
- *Fat: 18g*
- *Carbohydrates: 45g*
- *Protein: 5g*

Mug Caramel Apple Crisp

Ingredients:

- 1 small apple, peeled and diced
- 1/2 tablespoon lemon juice
- 1/2 tablespoon granulated sugar
- 1/4 teaspoon ground cinnamon
- 2 tablespoons rolled oats
- 1 tablespoon all-purpose flour
- 1 tablespoon brown sugar
- 1/2 tablespoon unsalted butter, melted
- Caramel sauce for topping
- Vanilla ice cream for serving

Method:

1. In a mug, toss diced apple with lemon juice, granulated sugar, and ground cinnamon.

2. In a separate bowl, mix rolled oats, flour, brown sugar, and melted butter.

3. Sprinkle the oat mixture over the apples in the mug.

4. Microwave on high for 2-3 minutes until the apples are tender.

5. Drizzle with caramel sauce and serve with vanilla ice cream.

Average Preparation Time: 7 minutes

Nutritional Information: (Approximate values per serving) - *Calories: 300 - Fat: 10g*

- *Carbohydrates: 50g - Protein: 2g*

CONCLUSION

As we reach the final pages of this mug recipes cookbook, I hope your culinary journey has been as delightful and satisfying as the meals you've created. Mug cooking isn't just a time-saving technique; it's a culinary adventure that empowers you to embrace creativity in the simplest of forms.

As you savor the last bites of your mug-made creations, remember that the beauty of these recipes lies in their accessibility. From busy professionals seeking a respite from hectic schedules to students navigating the demands of academia, mug meals have proven to be the ally of those who refuse to compromise on flavor despite life's fast pace.

In your hands, you hold more than just a collection of recipes; you have a toolkit for culinary spontaneity. The mug, once a humble vessel, has transformed into a canvas for your gastronomic imagination. From savory breakfasts that greet your day with warmth to indulgent desserts that cap it off with sweetness, each mug meal has been a celebration of simplicity and taste.

As you continue your culinary exploration, feel free to experiment, tweak, and make these recipes your own. Let this cookbook serve as a reminder that the joy of cooking knows no bounds, and a delicious, homemade meal is always within reach, even in the busiest of moments.

Thank you for joining me on this flavorful journey through the world of mug meals. May your mugs always be filled with creativity, and your meals be a reflection of the joy found in the art of cooking. Happy mug cooking!